Hija de mi padre

Solany Lara

ALEGRIA
PUBLISHING

Hija de mi padre
© 2023 Solany Lara
Impreso por: Alegría Publishing
Diseños de portada e interior: Josie Vasquez
Diseño: Diane Castañeda
Contacto: lara.solany@gmail.com

ISBN: 9798988174615

Library of Congress Control Number: 2023909002

Impreso en los Estados Unidos de América -
Printed in the United States of America

En la memoria de
a quien he tenido la dicha de llamar
mi padre:
Jose Francisco Lara.

Te amo y te extraño siempre.

Table of Contents

Foreword

My jaw dropped when I read the words written in the gratitude card I received, "She was unstoppable not because she did not have failures or doubts, but because she continued on despite them." I felt that Solany could see right through me. I worked so hard to hide my fears and struggles, and with that quote, I felt seen. She knew. This is when I first realized how connected Solany was with her world and the people around her. Her knowing was strong just like she shares in her poem, "Elevated:" "I feel deeply, but I also know deeply. I know before, after, and in the moment."

I met Solany during my time living in Los Angeles while working at Camino Nuevo Charter Academy in the McArthur Park neighborhood of Westlake. It's a community that is overflowing with Latinx culture, full of life, a community hustling and bustling, and populated with the most resilient humans. However, it's a community that has many needs and faces so many obstacles. Our work was never ending. In order to create programs that truly supported our scholars from kindergarten to 8th grade, we worked very closely with our coworkers. Solany became one of the coworkers I relied on for many aspects of my work. Many of our students needed support with their academics, social-emotional needs, and mental health. In order to show up to learn, our students needed love and patience, to be heard and to be seen. This came easy for Solany. She *saw* our kids. She *saw* our coworkers. She *saw* me.

I've worked in the education field for over 20 years. I've held many roles during my career: middle school teacher, parent coordinator, teacher assistant for special education, K-8 intervention teacher, and school administrator. I had the chance to work with many amazing educators and individuals that worked tirelessly to ensure a better future for our youth.

Solany is one of those amazing individuals I met during one of the toughest positions I've held as an educator. It was easy to show up and work hard for our community because of Solany and the many team members that came ready to give it their all. We became close friends and connected in many ways.

One thing you need to know about Solany is that she loves books more than anything in the world. She is always reading a few books at a time and always has a stack of books in line to be read. Books are one of her greatest weaknesses, as she will obsessively buy them, but they are also what give her strength. When she shared, she was going to write a poetry book dedicated to her late father, Jose Francisco Lara - I knew this was meant to be. I knew being a writer would be part of her path. It's so easy for Solany to connect with our humanity. She knows emotions and people, and she *really* knows books.

Solany's words in *Hija de mi padre* allows you to have an intimate look at what grief and loss feel like when losing a parent. Solany shares the beauty that her father held but also the challenges he faced. She shares an honest look at how machismo played a role in many aspects of her father's life, even at the end. She also touches on other difficult topics that are inevitable, such as the last days of life, afterlife responsibilities, how to show up when grief looms over you, including Mexican American culture issues. Some of her poems such as, "Pan dulce" and "Carcacha para metal" illuminate how grief highlights moments and things that seemed so mundane, but after losing your loved one, they become the most significant. Solany is able to show how grief forces you to reflect not only on your loved one's life, but on the lives of your ancestors too. Solany's touching words about grief will have you hold on to the things that matter the most just a little tighter.

In one of her poems, "Mi nombre," Solany shares a little about the meaning of her name. In this powerful line: "Sol que ilumina y aún brilla / después de la lluvia," I came to the realization of what *Hija de mi padre* represents: light and growth from darkness. In the past couple of years since her father's passing, Solany has been a guiding light for others that have lost a loved one. Solany was there for me when I lost my mother, Macaria, during the summer of 2021, a little over two years after she lost her father. Soon after mi Amá's passing, I received a care package with two books: a journal for grief and a memoir about losing your mom from cancer. The books were tender and touching. They helped me with all the emotions I was feeling. Solany knew exactly what I would be going through. She knew what I would need. This meant so much to me and still does. She was a beam of light during such a dark time. This is the reason it took me three tries to read *Hija de mi padre*. I couldn't get through one third of the poems before my eyes filled up with tears and I couldn't read anything. Solany's words helped me connect with my own experience with grief. It's comforting to know that these thoughts and feelings are not wrong nor that I'm alone.

I'm aware that if you're picking up this poetry book, you most likely have experienced grief from the loss of a loved one. First of all, I'm so sorry. Before reading this book of poetry, I highly recommend that you have some tissues handy. Lots of tissues. And definitely avoid reading it at a Panera Bread like I did. Soon after reading the first few poems, I found myself bawling and using up their napkins to wipe away my tears and mocos. I don't think anyone noticed.

Yesenia Puente Villalobos
Mother, Educator, & Remaker
Phoenix, Arizona

Preface

I'm a poet now.

The person who ignited my writing journey was my father, Jose Francisco Lara. "Chico," as many called him, was an esposo, father, hermano, son, tío, and friend who was Mexicano, alegre, passionate, caring, amoroso, enojón (a veces), a strict father, a self-proclaimed singer and dancer, and a great debater. I can't summarize my father in a few lines, but *Hija de mi padre* attempts in a variety of poetic forms and even provides a glimpse into who I was and am now after his death. This collection is my way of coping and communicating all the things I never said to mi padre. It's also a pathway to self-discovery as I transform into the woman and daughter I was meant to become because of what he taught me during his time on Earth.

This journey was ignited on April 20th, 2019, the day my dad passed due to complications from a stroke. After he left Earthside, I jumped into work, school, and socializing, believing that I had healed all the trauma wounds from his final months. I thought, *I need to get back to my routine, so I can move forward.* It felt like I was moving on, but when we were faced with COVID-19 lockdowns in March of 2020, I had no choice but to confront the reality: Dad wasn't here anymore. It was real and true. It felt heavier to be home facing my (our) new reality than to be outside of home. As a result, I faced my fears and thoughts alone, which often led to deep bouts of anxiety and depression. It was difficult to move forward without the first man I ever loved, especially at a time when life felt so uncertain.

During that time, I found myself in conflict with my family due to my decline in mental health, and I knew I was in desperate need of healing. I didn't know how, but knew I had to do something. Quickly. After a day I cried myself to sleep, I decided to attend a writing retreat hosted by Davina Ferreira because it couldn't possibly hurt to try something new. It didn't occur to me then that I would leave feeling so inspired. I felt more like the person I was before losing my father, and in that moment, I decided to write a poetry collection. I had no idea what it meant for me at that moment. I had written poetry during my Dad's hospital stay, but never thought myself a writer.

This was my leap of faith.

The tears I shed for mi padre led to me writing this collection, but I had no idea that it would provide healing, too. Now, I can say I'm a poet, writer, and healer. I hope that my writing can also help others heal. I hope my collection serves as a gift for mi familia y mis amigos. Although, what a gift it would be if my words could reach further than that. The possibility that my words may be able to resonate with others who have experienced something similar to me, whether it is: being a First-gen daughter, a Chicana, a grieving daughter, a woman transformed, or a daughter of immigrant parents. I hope it reaches the hands of many readers, but I'm also content knowing that I can give this book to mi mamá, mis hermanas, mis tíos, tías y primos.

Hija de mi padre is a journey of vulnerability into my lived experiences with my father and the transformation that comes with grief in both the light and the dark. The sun and light is present in a lot of my work because mi papá me nombró como el Sol. In contrast, darkness is grief, depression, and anxiety. Moreover, my collection is divided into two parts: *Recordando y llorando y Amando y brillando. Recordando y llorando* is mostly remembrance of who my father was and grieving him and the person I once was before experiencing death within my immediate family. *Amando y brillando* will lead you into poems about love in all the ways they exist in my life: family love, love for mis antepasados, and self-love after the rain. I recommend reading the collection in this order to connect fully, but each section has something to offer for any reader.

The thought of being in these shoes never occurred to me, but I'm glad that I have started this for myself first. Ya era tiempo de volar y seguir los sueños de la niña pequeña que se encerraba en su cuarto a leer todo el día. También ella se imaginaba ser una escritora y lo hizo. Se le olvidó ante el trauma que había vivido. Y ahora pienso, transformation is simply healing your inner child and coming back to those dreams that were forgotten due to traumatic experiences. Estoy contenta y estoy tan alegre de compartir un pedazo de mi vida, de mi padre y de mi corazón.

Solany Lara
Hija, Hermana, Amiga, y Poeta

The Light Within

Inside of me there is a light
that has been brought forth
by the shadows of my pages.

The pages have seen
not only the sunshine,
but also the sunset.

Where I've retracted mi luz from others,
the light has shone in my words.

It's not until people read these pages
that they will fully understand
that my light has always been present.

It just needed to be kept to myself
until I was ready to radiate again.

Recordando y llorando

Solany Lara

¿Cómo recordaré a papá?

Bailando hasta que ya no podía,
cantando hasta que los gallos se le salían.

Haciéndome la burla de tan chillona que me ponía,
asegurándose de que siempre hubiera comida.

Llamando a mi abuelita y a sus hermanos
que tanto quería.

Enseñándonos que nos amaba
con tantas cosas que él hacía.

Siempre viviendo para su familia.

Botas y tejana

El viejo Chico,
con sus botas y tejana.

Chico, Chicles,
Don Chico o "compa"
para todos.

Todos los ojos en él,
cuando entraba
a una fiesta.

Saludando a la gente
con su "OHT!"
y platicando hasta el atardecer.

Empezando la música
él zapateaba y cantaba

Siempre orgulloso
de ser él.

Nube Roja

We'd called him Red Cloud as code for:
Dad está enojado. Don't bother him right now.

He'd turn into Red Cloud
if we were too loud with our chisme
or our arguments for who didn't finish their chores.

Why didn't you take out the trash?
No one told me to do it.
Someone needs to tell you to take it out? Just do it!

Imagine his six girls yapping away
in la cocina after school.

You're so dumb!
Oh my God! Shut up!
You know you can help me, right?

I didn't realize how loud we'd get
until Dad's booming voice would say
¡Cómo chingan!
while he tried to watch his Mexican films.

He'd turn into Red Cloud
whenever he'd grow impatient with us
while we got ready for an outing.

Imagine his six girls sharing one bathroom
as they got ready for a family fiesta.

We'd say
Dad is turning red, ¡apúrense!

And, when we were making too much noise
while mom slept in
after a long night of work?

Forget about it!

Dad, huge looming Red Cloud,
would whisper-shout up the stairs,
¡Chingada madre, nomás que se despierte tu madre!

Red Cloud.

We'd use this name
when he wasn't terribly mad at us.

When he was extremely rojo,
we wouldn't have time to warn each other
or even think of joking.

He'd usually turn into Red Cloud
for good reason.

Because there really was no warning
for when he'd turn truly mad.

Grieving Out Loud

The worst is probably telling people I lost someone
because they don't know what to do with the information.

They stare at me
like I'm doing wrong by telling them.

It's as if I can't tell them
this part of my story.

Do they want me to hide
my dad and his death?

Then, I realize they probably haven't lost someone dear to them
or they have learned to suppress their emotions.

So, I just tell them to enjoy the time
they have with their loved ones
because that's probably all they can understand
at this moment.

Pan dulce

As I woke up for school,
I could count on seeing Dad at the table
with his pan dulce and café con leche.

It was his routine.
To enjoy the sweetness of a concha, oreja, o elote
as he watched the morning news play on Univision.

He'd savor every drop
of the piping hot coffee he poured to the brim
as he waited for my sisters and I to get ready to go.

It was a moment all for himself,
where he didn't have to hear
the screams of his six girls

fighting with each other
or having to share the televisión.
A moment

where he didn't need to work hard
to put food on the table,
to buy us the next outfit or school supplies.

His moment
to take in the day
before a long workday.

The Entire World Sitting on my Shoulders

The pressure of the world
can be so debilitating–
so much so that it feels as if I'm carrying the entire world
on my back, como El Mundo de la Lotería.

My shoulders, neck, and back tire out
under the weight of all my worries,
trapped beneath them for days without anyone knowing.

Stuck,
drowning,
with no way out.

Recycling Bins

Our recycling bins were always full.

It was either Coca Cola
or Dad's endless beer cans and bottles
piling up high into the sky.

The glass bottles clinked against each other
and the aluminum cans crunched
as he finished drinking his share for the day.

Some bottles and cans never made it into the bins,
laid sprawled around like avocado leaves under the tree.

Much the same,
Dad's drinking wasn't a problem until it started to show up
outside the recycling bins.

Until Dad shouted at mom.
Until Dad threw the television to the ceramic floor.
Until Dad struggled to make it to bed without our help.
Until Dad got locked out of the house.
Until Dad hurled himself out of a moving car.
Until Dad tried to knock a room door down.
Until Dad was questioned by the police.
Until Mom cried in the living room.

Until,
his body
couldn't handle
being without alcohol.

Árbol de aguacate

Las hojas de aguacate bailan de izquierda a derecha
y me traen recuerdos de cuando papá bailaba debajo del árbol.

Lo hacía para hacerme reír después de un largo día
bajando los aguacates y barriendo las hojas caídas.

Era como su celebración al terminar el día de cosecha.

A pesar de que apá ya no está en este mundo terrenal,
el árbol de aguacate sigue dando su flor.

Decisión

He decidido que te perdonaré,
lo decidí porque nunca aprendiste
a desahogarte sin tomar.

Yo, tuve el privilegio de poder
encontrar otras maneras de hacerlo.
Y por eso, estoy agradecida contigo.

Sin tenerte papá, yo no sería yo.

Calls to México

Even though mi papá had the privilege
to come from México to the U.S. for a better life,

he never forgot his roots. He never forgot
his madre or his padre; he never forgot

his hermanos, his hermanas, his tías, or his tíos.
Always making calls while drinking

to transport himself there. Until he had a chance
to return home: where he always truly longed to be.

Trips to Mexico

One-lane roads took us from Nogales to Jalisco
as we passed a volcano and drove in foggy weather.

The fear of being stopped by police always on our mind
porque uno nunca sabe las intenciones de una parada.

We'd stop by Oxxos for botana
y tacos en cada ciudad.

Mom sat in the passenger seat
telling us - *¡Ya mero!* - even if it wasn't true.

As dad drove in the pitch black roads,
mis hermanas y yo slept in the back of the astro van.

We'd wake to the sun rising,
and finally get word we were about to get the carretera
hacia Santa Cruz de las Flores.

We'd arrive at Mama Soco's casita,
and slide the door open to jump out
and run to her door.

Llegábamos y estaban todos
los tíos, tías, primos y primas
para recibirnos con los brazos abiertos.

¡Hija, qué bueno que llegaron bien!

Abrazos y besos
por aquí y por allá.

Hija de mi padre

Conversaciones y carcajadas
hasta la madrugada.

Jugando Bote Pateado
con todos los niños de la vecindad.

Escondiéndonos en los techos de las casas
y los carros abiertos de los vecinos.

También había el juego de Basta,
donde uno tenía que escribir
un nombre, apellido, animal, fruta/flor y cosa
antes que todos los demás.

El pueblo en el que aprendimos
"Allá en el Chile Verde" con las primas.

Había una señorita bailando cha, cha, cha.
Cha…Cha…Cha.
Olé…Olé…Olé.
Y chapí, chapí, chapí.
Arriba la cafetera,
cafetera de marfil.

Fiestas con banda en la plaza
y andar a caballo en el rancho.

Al cruzar de la casa de Mamá Soco,
donde cenábamos tacos todas las noches.

Regresando a Estados Unidos
con libras de más
en nuestra maleta, panza y corazón.

El amor de mi padre a mi madre

Casi se tiraba de un balcón para proclamar su amor por ella.
Mandaba a los niños de la vecindad para que ella saliera de casa.
La sacaba a bailar danzón mientras la banda tocaba.
Le daba besos y abrazos mientras ella limpiaba.
Dejaba que ella durmiera hasta las doce de la tarde.
Construía, pintaba y arreglaba toda la casa.
Cocinaba desayuno por la mañana y se lo llevaba a su cama.
Llenaba el tanque de gas del carro antes de que ella trabajara.
Le regalaba anillos o medallas de oro en cada evento especial.
Le cantaba en cada fiesta (con o sin músicos en vivo).

Así fue como mi padre demostró el amor que le tenía a mi madre.

Astro Van

Él esperaba
en el white astro van
a su reina y a sus seis tesoros.

Fumaba con enojo
cuando no se apresuraban,
pero aún esperaba.

El astro van
se llenaba de voces
alegando a dónde ir:
Hija, ¿a la izquierda o a la derecha?,
¡Apá, derecho no derecha!

Con él logramos viajar
a nuestro México lindo y querido.

Navegando como familia,
a la próxima fiesta o a Disneylandia.

Todos alegando
en el camino,
hasta llegar al destino.

En nuestro
Astro van.

Carcacha para Metal

Ding, clang, boom.

I could hear my dad
coming from miles away
for me at my bus stop.

Metal rubbing and hitting against each other,
as his gray carcachita
hit bumps on the road.

Ding, clang, boom.

The first time he showed us
his new unemployment venture,
I was embarrassed, but my dad had no shame at all.

He was proud of his carcacha
because it allowed him
to be his own jefe.

Ding, clang, boom.

He'd work hard
picking up anything metal
for miles beyond.

He even asked us to help him write:
"Pick up Metal"
with his número de cel.

Ding, clang, boom

Hija de mi padre

He'd get home exhausted
from lifting heavy metal
and sometimes all cut up.

His body grew tired
and his mind stressed
because he felt he wasn't making enough.

Ding, clang, boom.

He threw hurtful words at my mom
because he could not grow used to her
being the breadwinner.

Ding,
clang,
boom,

Went a blood clot in his brain.

I no longer hear the *ding, clang, boom*
from the metal but oh,
how many times I've wanted to hear it again.

Death is Trauma

I used to think that a traumatic death
was one where you had to see blood, gore, or several people
hurt.

Dad's death made me realize that any death is trauma.
The upheaval of your entire life in a single moment.

Nothing is the same as it once was, and it will never be again.

That's trauma–
your life is forever changed–

> A single moment.
> A single day.
> A single death.

It changes you.

Realm of Grief

When someone loses a loved one
they are lost to a completely different realm.

Lost in their thoughts, stuck in the past:
in the should've, could've, would've.

It's almost as if they're trying to reach out for them
on the other side. Asking themselves constantly:

Why did this happen? How could this be?
Why me? What could I have done differently?

Playing out different scenarios that might have resulted
in different outcomes. Only to come back to

the same conclusion.

The Love He Gave Us

My dad couldn't give me brand named clothing,
but he'd take me to Skechers at Huntington Park
before the new school year.

My dad wouldn't make an American breakfast in the mornings,
but he would share half of his steaming bean, egg,
and chile torta as he drove me to my bus stop.

My dad didn't have the nicest car,
but I knew he was coming to pick me up
when I heard metal rattling against each other.

My dad didn't pay for caterers for our family parties,
but he would make the most delicious birria ever.

My dad wouldn't pay for our house to get fixed,
instead he would fix everything himself.

My dad wouldn't take my mom out for brunch every weekend,
but he would bring *McDonals Deluxe Breakfast* for her in bed.

My dad couldn't take us to different parts in the world,
but he would take us to museums in Los Angeles
and to Santa Cruz de las Flores, Jalisco.

He was the best dad.

Despite all odds,
despite all circumstances,
and despite not being rich.

He did what he could with what he had:
with love, patience,
and a whole lot of discipline.

Now,
I will take all the love he gave me,
and do what I can.

Papá

Tu vida no ha sido fácil,
cruzaste la frontera pensando
las cosas serían diferente aquí,
pero nada cambió.

Siempre trabajando,
siempre luchando
y siempre bebiendo.

Sin embargo,
has sido el mejor papá
para mí.

30 de Marzo

A day
I'll never
                forget.

This day was not only
traumatizing for me,
                but I know that for you it was, too.

Yet,
you consoled me,
                as doctors roamed around you.

Connecting you
                to machines
                and running multiple tests on you.

I just stared
                feeling dumbfounded,
                                helpless, scared.

I should have consoled you.

But instead,
you locked eyes with me
and told me,

                ¿Hija, todo va a estar bien.
                ¿Para qué te asustas?

I tried to
                snap out
                                of it

as difficult as it was
because I needed
to step in
to translate
everything
the doctors were telling me
to tell you.

You were so scared;
I could see it
in your eyes.

Yet,
you still tried
to be the best father
you could be
in that moment,
on that day.

Passing the Torch

No one prepared me for the death of my father.
It just happened. One day,

he was here until he suddenly was not.
I was expected to hold it together

for the sake of others. Often being told
that I have to be stronger for my younger sister and mother.

Completely unprepared for the countless responsibilities
mi padre once had. I often feel like he did

because I seem to not be giving, doing, being
enough. I find myself repeating:

I'm not my father, I'm his daughter.
I don't have to be everyone's savior.
They can save themselves.

Aguantando la respiración

Sin respiracion me la llevo
cuando tengo mil cosas
  que hacer,
   lugares que estar
   y tanto que dar.

¿Cómo suspiro entre todo esto?

Delete/Restore

To delete the pictures of mi apá
while he was in the hospital
or not to delete?

A question that comes up
when I stumble upon them.

They were the blurred moments
that suddenly come rushing in as I scroll
through my "Dad" photos folder on my iPhone.

There is the picture of him
I had sent to my nurse sister
to see if I should call the ambulance.

The pictures I took
to send to my sisters
when it was my turn to stay with him.

Every time I happen to see them,
I relive the pain of him
tied to tubes and the hospital bed.

I delete only to restore.
Finding myself wanting to keep
every fragment of him while he was on this Earth.

But then, I spiral into a realm of grief
and question whether I'm doing the right thing.

I don't know what is right anymore.

All I know
is that grief is damn hard.

The Doing and Being Enough

The doing never seems like enough.
Overworking with no end in sight
just to make ends meet.

Tengo main job
y también side hustles,
pero nunca es suficiente.

Studying because it will get
the job that fills the cup,
but the end never seems in sight.

Trying to keep up
with family and friends,
the pets, chores y el novio.

Pero,
when to find time
to descansar?

Yo solo quiero *ser*.
No expectations,
just *ser*.

> Resting deeply.
> Reading with no time constraints.
> Dancing without worries.
> Writing freely.
> Loving myself fully.

Can this be enough?
Will I let others down just for being me?

Maybe,
but I will only feel enough
when I choose *me* amongst the doing.

- Uno no puede lucir como el sol si no descansa como la luna.

Flight

Anything that feels just like Dad's passing,
out of my control, makes me want to run.

Since then, I feel like taking flight from my problems,
from conflict, from anything that is too overwhelming.

Flight.
My response to trauma.

I've come to realize this has always been my way to respond:

> fleeing to my room to read and escape the endless
> arguments, throwing myself into work and studies to
> conceal anxiety, writing a poetry collection to cope

Not horrible things, but sometimes I don't think people realize
that I'm not trying to disappear from their lives.

I'm just trying to get away
from my own thoughts.

And, people just need to let me soar
as I figure it all out for myself.

I need all the space, support, and therapy to do so.
But most of all, time.

Worn Out

As a child,
life was a gem
with no clock in mind.

Getting older wore the gem down,
with the sound of the hand ticking
louder and louder.

El machismo mata

Notamos la tristeza en sus ojos,
el enojo de más y como el alcohol lo consumió.

Le dijimos que viera un terapeuta, que fuera a rehabilitación
o al médico. Eventualmente, eso se volvió

a rogar y llorar. Tratamos de razonar con él,
a un lado de nuestros aliados: nuestros tíos, esposos o novios.

Mientras tanto, él nos insultaba y decía:
¿cómo me voy a dejar mandar por ellas?

Tratamos de sostenerlo mientras caía,
pero su orgullo era más grande que todos nosotros.

Rechazó nuestra ayuda y en cambio,
construyó una pared de botellas. Nuestras palabras

ya no eran suficientes, nada funcionó. Nuestra paciencia
se agotó y lo recibimos con la misma irá, con la que él nos recibía.

Y pronto todo eso se convertiría en luto.

¿Podríamos haber hecho más?
¿Hacer las cosas de manera diferente?
¿Qué más se podía hacer?

Tarde nos dimos cuenta
que su machismo no le dejaba buscar ayuda.

El machismo mató a mi papá, porque su orgullo
fue mayor que dejar que su esposa e hijas lo ayudaran,
cuando él se sentía lo más bajo en la vida.

Cuando bajo el sol

I wish I could get back to who I was before losing you.
Life no longer makes sense.

I find myself lost in my thoughts more often
than in the present. My concentration lasts a second

before I think of you or even think of me.
Why can't I move on?

I'm stuck on this rollercoaster ride of emotions.
My screams stay in my head with nowhere to go.

I want to run away and let go.
This weight on my heart is suffocating me to no end.

I want to find a way back to being me:
careless and healthy. Please help me.

I want to get back to shining bright like the sun I once was,
but I need all the warmth of those around me to continue on.

Running Out of Time

We don't realize how our time is so limited
until we lose someone.

Before that, it seemed as if time was endless,
but death comes knocking at the door

and suddenly time defines everything.
Defies everything.

There doesn't seem to be enough time
to love those around you.

It seems like there is never enough time
in the day to accomplish everything.

The time you spend relaxing
seems like a waste.

There is a feeling that at any moment
you may lose someone.

Time is lost worrying and obsessing,
not really spent being present.

Sin pelos en la lengua

There were times I wanted to hide and melt away
when Dad would say something sin filtro —
which was almost 100% of the time.

What he thought,
he'd say without shame.

I always admired the confidence,
but sometimes, I wished Dad would think
before he spoke.

Not everyone could take his humor like we did,
but Dad didn't care.

Those that didn't like it stopped coming around,
and those that stuck around
were there when things began to go South.

They saw my dad high and low.
They were able to meet him with the same: no filtro,
called him out on his behavior.

That's the good thing about being without pelos en la lengua.
Tell it like it is.

Except dad couldn't take it from us.
Just from the men.

How to Love Someone Through the Grief

Offer your shoulder to cry on when they can't
seem to hold the tears in. Understand that

they're not angry at you; they are angry at themselves,
the circumstances, or God. Give them

the space they need to process that they must exist
without the one they're grieving. Release

the time frame you have for them because grief
has no timeline. Allow them

to find their way back to life again. Receive them
with open arms when they're ready to face the world.

Repeat as needed.

Silence is Deadly

I write and talk about death
because people don't speak about it enough.

They don't talk about how traumatic it can be
and how life-changing it is.

They don't talk about how grieving people
need space held for them,
need space to process,
and need more time.

Always more time.

They don't talk about the endless responsibilities
that come with death:
making decisions over their loved one's memories and belongings,
finding a place to bury their loved one,
choosing how to bury them
and what to bury them in.

Nobody can prepare
for how to move on with life after death.

More people should be speaking about it,
but no one likes to listen
about something that eventually will come for them.

However, I know that the only way to get through
is to be open about it because someone may be struggling
with this, too.

And, silence,
silence, can be deadly.

The Last Days

Before my dad's last day,
I held the darkness in his face
because I knew he had so much light to give.

Many times
this is what I wished
I had done differently.

Instead of holding the pitch black,
I should have held beams of light
towards him.

Showing him
that I took after
the name he gave me.

Instead, I detracted my light
because all I saw
was his darkness.

When he passed onto the other side,
it dawned on me that he was scared of the dark,
unaware of how to overcome it.

It was too much
to bear for someone who was proud of
being the man of the house.

Un machista to no end,
who knew no better way to deal with his darkness
other than keeping it all to himself.

Desbordándome

Doing too much doesn't feel like enough,
when you're not met with the same enough.

People take and take,
but don't realize that I need more.

Keep your material possessions.
I don't need those.

I need support,
encouragement,
and love.

Where are my words of affirmation
when I always try to shine them onto others
like the rays of the sun?

I fear my warmth will give out. How much more
can I take, being taken from,
before my rays go dim?

Chillona

I've always been what my dad would call me
every time I would cry:
una chillona.

Mi familia always made me feel like it was a bad thing,
and this made me believe it was:
a weakness, a flaw, and a bother.

¡Quiere llorar, quiere llorar!
would regularly be repeated to me
as tears dropped to my lap.

I was the center of everyone's jokes
because I was so quick to break
during an argument.

Didn't they notice
I just needed someone's comfort
to tell me that everything would be fine?

I cried because the arguing
made me nervous.

I needed reassurance
that I was not a disappointment
for one single thing I had done wrong (not even crying).

No one noticed that the tears were a river of my own
to clear the emotions I felt
when no one came to shine their warmth on me.

Hija de mi padre

Me sanaba con mis propias lágrimas,
no me quedaba de otra.
I at least had a way to release all the pressure.

My dad on the other hand
was constantly consumed in his own thoughts,
never letting out his fears and emotions.

He instead chose
to sit with beers in hand
to drown his sorrows.

Never telling us
how he also needed reassurance
to know everything would be okay.

That he needed us
to also be there to lift him up,
and did not need to carry everything on his own.

After his death,
I saw the strength en mis lágrimas
because they showed me that all along
I was crying all the tears my dad couldn't.

Running Out of Breath

In the moment I saw my dad struggle for breath,
I, too, felt like I struggled to breathe.

A huge weight pressing in
around me.

Without anywhere to go,
I felt like running away from the unfathomable.

The end of my dad's life.

It was too much to bear seeing him there
without the power to make him feel better.

So, like a coward, I ran from his hospital room
while he struggled with his last breath.

I wish I could take that moment back.
I wish I had chosen to stay in the room with him.
I wish I had been at his side to console him.
I wish I had done a lot of things differently.

I hope he knows that now.

Not So Macho After All

In some ways, Dad was machista,
and in others, not so much. He wouldn't refuse

to cook for his girls and his wife. He'd step into the kitchen
with pride, ready to cook if Mom could not.

If we told him: "¡Apá, ocupamos más toallas femeninas!"
He'd zoom out the door to the store.

He wouldn't bat an eye when people saw him unloading his cart
with multiple packs of feminine products.

He'd get many sneers and side-eyed looks of,
"Why is he even buying pads?"

Mom hardly stepped into the grocery store
because he'd go before she even got to it.

We thought this was normal,
but when Dad did this in Mexico

todos decían: *¡Ay, qué mandilón!*

I Choose to Let the River Flow

In a culture that chooses not to show emotion,
I choose to let my tears flow freely.

I choose to let them run their course
so there could be light.

I choose to teach the next generation
that tears do not mean weakness.

I choose to show the current generation
what could be if you cleanse this way:

> After the rain comes the shine
> It hurts less if you let it all out
> It does not need to be done behind closed doors
> In doing so, you give space to others to do the same
> Men cry too, and probably need it the most

And, perhaps allowing the river to flow freely
will allow us to flow more easily with one another

Imagine that.

Busco Sol-edad

Quiero estar sola durante este tiempo,
porque siento que mi luz se va apagando.

Estoy tratando de proteger el fuego
que llevo dentro de mí.

Especialmente
durante este invierno.

Donde la luz del sol se siente menos
y la oscuridad llega antes.

Siento que también la oscuridad se lleva mi luz
y no quiero eso.

Voy a retirar mi luz hasta que sienta
que pueda alumbrar de nuevo
como el Sol que yo soy.

El sazón de papá

Everyone knew
that my dad's food
era muy deliciosa.

Tortas de huevo
con chile y frijoles
dripping from the sides.

Carnitas y cueritos
crackling
in the cazo.

Menudo waking us
with its pungent smell
as he cooked it throughout the early morning.

Tacos al estiló Jalisco,
con chile bien picosito
y tortillas dipped en aceite de carne asada.

Birria cooked
with tons of spices y chiles,
con consomé para chuparse los dedos.

Hasta gente le pedía
que cocinara para fiestas
y todos trataban de averiguar la famosa receta.

We try to make his dishes,
but his sazón and love are missing.

Couldn't Be Me Without You

I'm aware of my privilege:
an education, a job,
and all that makes me
who I am today.

You didn't have many of the experiences I have:

> parents who put education first,
> money to pay for that education,
> exposure to different cultures and ways of thinking,
> and examples of what healthy communication looks like.

I know you and mamá did your best.

I want you to know your hard work and tenacity,
despite all odds against you,
is wholeheartedly seen
and appreciated by me.

Because I couldn't
be me
without you
> … being you.

Primera Generación

Aunque descanso como el sol,
tengo tanta pasión por dentro para entregar al mundo.

Cuando trato de apagarme, me siento ansiosa.
Siento que no estoy poniendo lo suficiente de mi parte

en el legado de la familia. Me siento como, "muy selfish."
Pero, ¿acaso no saben que esta carga es demasiada?

Necesito un poco de self-care para seguir luchando.
Un poco de paciencia, amor, y apoyo

para seguir dando. Porque no solo lucho por mí,
lucho por: mi madre, mi padre, mis hermanas, mis tíos,

mis primos, mis abuelos, mis bisabuelos, y todos
los que vinieron antes de mí.

Y eso es demasiado...

Solamente
            necesito
                        momentos
                                    para mi.

El Rey

Mi papá se sentía muy rey
cuando escuchaba
a Chente.

Cuando tomaba tequila,
soltaba el llanto
mientras escuchaba sus canciones.

Escucha: "Mi viejo"- Vicente Fernández

Cada vez que cantaba "Mi viejo,"
Chente lo acompañaba en el luto por su querido padre,
mi abuelo Pancho.

Cuando estábamos en una fiesta con mariachi en vivo,
mi padre tomaba el escenario
como si fuera el rey.

Le cantaba a mi madre
sus canciones de amor
en frente de todos.

Escucha: "Las llaves de mi alma"- Vicente Fernández

Yo me quedaba admirando a mi papá
como si fuera todo un artista
cuando él soltaba un grito:
¡AAAaaaaaaaaaaaaay, ay, aya y ay!

Ahora cuando escucho las canciones de Vicente,
él también me acompaña en mi luto
porque me recuerda a mi padre,
Jose Francisco Lara, Chico, dad, papá.

Escucha: "El Hombre Que Más Te Amó"- Vicente Fernández

Cantando

En los momentos que canto
te recuerdo.

Puede que mi voz
no esté tan afinada como la tuya,
pero porque pienso en ti puedo elevarla.

Me regalaste el sentido de confianza
en quién realmente soy yo:
el poder de mi nombre y de aquellos que me precedieron.

Sin tener miedo de ser escuchado,
tu reclamabas a gritos quién eras
y nos cantabas con el amor que un padre tiene por sus hijas.

A veces, no escuchábamos el amor en tus canciones,
por que estábamos demasiado concentradas
en el sonido de tu voz atronadora
en lugar de lo que querías decirnos.

No nos dábamos cuenta
de que te preocupabas por nuestro bien.

No porque no confiabas en nosotras,
sino porque no confiabas en el mundo.

No te escuchaba entonces,
pero ahora te escucho.

Te escucho:
en los momentos en que estoy caminando sola,
cuando alguien se quiere aprovechar de mi,
y también en los momentos que siento que ya no puedo más.

También en el viento,
en las canciones que cantaste fuerte,
y en el vaivén de las hojas de nuestro árbol de aguacate.

Te recuerdo y recuerdo quién soy yo:
una mujer fuerte que eleva su voz
como le enseñó su padre.

Lo que soy gracias a mi padre

Chillona pero chingona.
Chingona cuando recuerdo lo que me enseñó.

Me enseñó:

> Eres Sol
> Sé fuerte
> Baila hasta que la música deje de sonar
> Mi casa es tu casa
> Ama sin temor

Con todo esto y gracias a él,
pude ver lo brillante e inspiradora que soy yo.

Canciones de la infancia

Hay algunas canciones
que simplemente me transportan
a momentos de mi infancia.

Antes de darme cuenta,
vuelvo a ser chiquita y las memorias vienen otra vez
como si mi mente estuviera regresando los casetes VHS.

Juan Gabriel y Rocío Dúrcal cantando "Te Quiero Mucho
Mucho"
me recuerda a papá tratando de bailar con mamá en la cocina,
mientras ella limpiaba.

Vicente Fernandez cantando "Las Mañanitas"
despertándonos por la mañana
y papá abrazándonos para felicitarnos.

Los Tigres del Norte cantando "Mi Linda Esposa"
que papá ponía tan fuerte
para despertar a mamá en el Día de San Valentín.

Paquita la del Barrio cantando "Rata de Dos Patas"
cuando mamá estaba enojada con papá
y se la pasaba sin hablar con él.

Chelo cantando "La Lámpara"
y mamá cantando mientras limpiaba
pensando que nadie la escuchaba.

Rocio Durcal cantando la canción "Amor Eterno"
en el estereo del carro de mi tío Carlos,
rumbo a mi casa, después de una pijamada con prima Vero.

Esa canción me regresa al presente y me despierta
con un significado completamente diferente para mí:

> *Cómo quisiera, !ay!*
> *Que tú vivieras*
> *Que tus ojitos jamás se hubieran*
> *Cerrado nunca y estar mirándolos*

after songwriter,
> *Juan Gabriel*

Oht!

Oht, decía él
cuando se encontraba
con todos.

Oht, era su manera
de decir: ¿qué tal?

Oht al vecino.
Oht a sus compadres.
Oht a sus compañeros de trabajo.

Oht, eres bienvenido.

Ya no

Lo más difícil de perder una persona
es cambiar el presente a pasado.

Ya no puedo decir:
> "Mi papá *es…*"
Ahora tengo que decir:
> "Mi papá *era…*"

Ya no puedo esperarlo en frente de nuestra casa
con una ceja parada para recibirme.

Ya no puedo reírme porque se durmió
en el comedor viendo cine mexicano.

Ya no puedo escuchar su voz profunda
al cruzar la casa.

Ya no puedo celebrar mi cumpleaños con él
como siempre lo hacíamos.

Ya no puedo bailar con él
en todas las fiestas familiares.

Ya no puedo escucharlo gritar: "Sol"
cuando él ocupaba de mi ayuda.

Ya no estará aquí para ver
estos poemas que fueron escritos para él.

Y sin embargo yo sé,
que él sigue conmigo
en espíritu y alma.

Y es por eso, que he podido hacer todo
lo que mi corazón desea.

I Don't See You in My Dreams

Since we lost you,
I don't see you in my dreams
like my sisters have.

You've never visited me
while I'm asleep, and for a while,
I was upset that it has never been the case,
only to eventually realize
that you visit me while I'm awake.

I feel you the strongest
      when I write,
      when I honor you,
      when I remember the good times,
      when I reflect on all the bad,
      when I notice I'm falling into the same patterns.

You are with me.
Guiding me.
Siempre.

Resting Rate

Often I feel like it's a violation
of the law of physics
to be at a resting rate.

Now, I'm taking all the rest I need
to push forward against
the gravity of the world.

A world that demands
more and more,
without time to catch my breath.

Oxygen is needed to flow like water
amidst the mountains pushing against me.

So I tell myself:

Breathe. Flow.

Hasta Luego

It felt like a goodbye,
but then memories remind me
it's a see you by and by.

Tears drop each time,
but then a smile
suddenly withholds me.

I feel your presence within me,
no longer feeling
without you, Dad.

Papá, un año.

Papá, de pequeño, posando con una pistola.

Papá y Tío Ángel con traje militar, para llevar
las banderas durante un desfile escolar.

Papá con otro niño (desconocido) y su padrino,
durante la primera comunión.

Papá con su clase, en la escuela primaria.

Papá, identificación escuela primaria, 1974.

Papá con el abuelo Pancho, el día de su boda, 1982.

Papá y mamá, tomando la comunión durante
la ceremonia de su boda, 1982.

Papá y tío Rigoberto (su hermano mayor),
el día de sus bodas compartidas,1982.

Papá, en sus veinte.

Papá, cantando con mariachi.

Papá tomando una cerveza con un amigo
en un bar, San José.

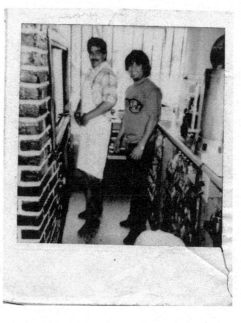

Papá con un compañero, en uno de sus primeros
trabajos en un restaurante en San Jose, California.

Papá con su madre y todos sus hermanos. Dejaron un espacio
en el medio para luego insertar al abuelo Pancho.

Mamá en medio de sus dos jefes de
uno de sus primeros trabajos.

Mamá, a la derecha de una amiga
para un evento especial.

Mamá relajándose en un sofá.
Probablemente alrededor de la década de 1980.

Papá y mamá, en el parque.

Mamá con mi hermana mayor, Carla.

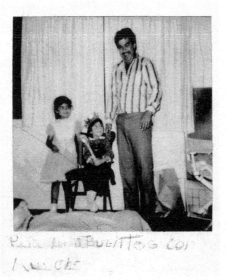

Papá con hermanas mayores, Carla y Amanda. El reverso de la imagen dice: "Con mucho cariño para mis abuelitos. Aquí recordamos el 15 de septiembre: El día del grito. Coronamos la reina del pueblo y también echamos el grito".

Papá con mis tres hermanas mayores, Carla, Amanda
y María, en su primera residencia en San José,
después de emigrar a los EE. UU.

Papá haciendo de caballo con Mary y Amanda encima
y Carla comiendo elote en el parque.

Una salida familiar en la noche de Halloween en
Los Angeles. Soy el bebe en la carriola.

Papá y mamá en la misa de quince de Carla.

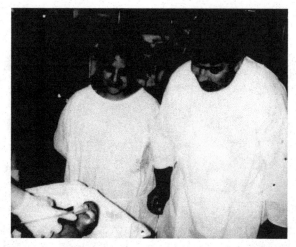

Papá y mamá miran y sonríen a la bebé prematura Coraly (una de las gemelas) en el conocido Hospital de Mujeres y Niños en el Este de Los Ángeles, 1996.

Papá y tío Carlos en la Nochevieja de 2002.

Toda nuestra familia para la reunión de cumpleaños
de Carla.

Papá, mamá y las gemelas en su ceremonia
de misa de quince.

Las hermanas Lara-Martínez para el Baby Shower temático de los Dodgers de María, de izquierda a derecha: Coraly, Carla, María, Solany, Amanda y Marely.

Graduación de mi bachillerato de California State University, Stanislaus 2017. De izquierda a derecha: María (tercera hermana mayor), mamá, papá, yo, Yamiseli (sobrina-hija de Carla) y Carla (hermana mayor).

Mamá, papá y yo para la graduación de mi bachillerato de California State University, Stanislaus, 2017.

Mamá y papá bailando durante la fiesta de cumpleaños número 60 de mamá.

Papá y mi segunda hermana mayor, Amanda.

Papá y mi tercera hermana mayor, Mary en
Tenno Sushi.

Papá y una de las hermanas gemelas, Coraly, en su
graduación de la escuela secundaria.

Papá y una de las hermanas gemelas, Marely, en
Disneyland.

Papá y mamá con su nieta, Yamiseli.

Papá con su nieto, David.

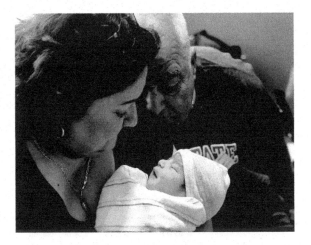

Mamá y Papá con su nieto, Adrián.

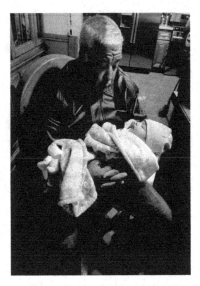

Papá con su nieto, Julián.

Papá con dos de sus hermanas.
A la izquierda, Estela. A la derecha, Leticia.

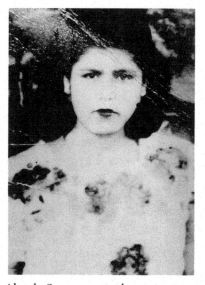

Abuela Socorro cuando era joven o como
preferimos llamarla: Mamá Soco.

Abuela Agustina y su hijo Héctor.

Los padres de mi mamá: Abuela Agustina y
Abuelo Jesús.

Un retrato de toda la familia de mi papá que mi mamá le regaló para uno de sus cumpleaños. Arriba: Tío Jesús, Papá, Tío Ramón y Tío Carlos. En medio: Tía Estela, Abuelo Pancho, Abuela Soco y Tío Rigoberto. Abajo: Tía Lilia, Tía Patricia, Tío Memo, Tío Ángel y Tía Leticia.

Abuela Agustina con su atuendo mexicano para
celebrar las fiestas patrias.

Amando y brillando

Light and Darkness

Sometimes, more than we care to admit,
we let our gloom overshadow
the brilliance of life–

walking deeper into the endless dark.

Deeper and deeper, darker and darker,
we ignore the rays of life;
we forget what illuminates us.

But daily, the Earth reminds us
that the sun still comes up
even after a starless night.

It's only by searching for pockets of sunshine
that we are able
to find ourselves again.

We must rise,
despite the darkness.

Mi nombre

Mi nombre es un recuerdo
de mi padre.

Él, me nombró
como el sol.

Sol que ilumina y aún brilla
después de la lluvia.

Un recuerdo de quién realmente soy:
hija de mi padre.

Azul

As the clouds cleared from the sky,
I began to see azul.

Azul came into my life and helped me
see that life wasn't just clouds

and rain thundering down. I could see
the light again, and take comfort

that the azul from the sky would still be there
even if I have cloudy days.

Siguiendo los rayos de luz

Vuelvo a mí cuando me doy cuenta que honrar mi voz
es más importante que las voces de afuera.

Vuelvo a mí cuando escucho mis latidos
y mis propios pensamientos.

Sigo mis sueños
sin pensar en lo que digan los demás.

Sigo los rayos de luz
entre toda la oscuridad.

Y me encuentro volviendo a mí.

La Chinga

De nada mis padres hicieron oro y plata,
era una chinga para los dos,

pero lo hicieron. Lo hicieron sin una educación,
sin papeles y hasta con seis hijas.

Yo me quejo por un día de chinga.
Era una chinga, pero ellos lo hicieron con más peso

sobre sus espaldas. Y pues, me levanto y sigo,
sigo por mí, por ellos y por mi familia.

Porque ellos me recuerdan que vengo
de una familia de luchadores.

Luchadores hasta el fin.

A la vida

Gracias a la vida
por las lecciones que me ha dado.
Tiempo, tiempo y otra vez.

Sin reprocharme,
me recibe con los brazos abiertos
cada vez que me encuentro sin ganas de vivir.

Y aunque yo
le he reclamado,
ella me dice:

ven y vive.

Family Portraits

"Mi casa, es tu casa," mi papá would say.

Our house covered with family portraits
shows you the extent of our family's past.

My dad stands tall in a retrato across the entrance,
welcoming you into the house he renovated by hand.

On the opposite wall hangs the painted portrait of Los Lara:
mi papá con sus hermanas, hermanos
y también mis abuelos: Papá Pancho y Mamá Soco.

Los ancestros that loved and guided
with what they could and what they knew.

Another surface carries the wedding picture
that started the present generation: a young mom and dad
con su hija mayor acompañándolos en su matrimonio.

Y las hijas Lara que vinieron después,
en cada esquina y cada rincón:
enseñando el orgullo de la madre.

En las mesas y libreros están la siguiente generación:
los nietos y la nieta que llenan la casa con risas;
listos para seguir sus sueños.

Estos retratos te hacen sentir que no estás solo,
y quizá, tú también eres parte de esta familia mexicana.

Otra historia más contribuyendo
a la trayectoria de inmigrantes Latinos en Estados Unidos.

Porque estás en casa y estamos unidos
con el mismo sueño que nos trajo aquí.

Elevated

I'm a highly sensitive person.
I thought it was a bad thing when I was chiquita.

Ahora, como adulta, I find that it's a gift.
My intuition is elevated.

I feel deeply, but I also know deeply.
I know before, after, and in the moment.

I hear everything even when people don't know it.

A tear drops? I'm there.
You need to talk? I'm there.
You need support? I'm there.

Sometimes without realizing it,
but I'm there.

Mamá Soco

Nuestra abuela,
nuestra paloma blanca
crió once hijos:
siete varones y cuatro hembras.

Lo logró con Papá Pancho,
y todavía me pregunto:
¿cómo lograron hacerlo?

Los nietos y bisnietos
tienen la dicha
de todavía tenerla aquí.

Su pelo es blanco,
camina con pasitos
y también ataca con cosquillas.

Cuando la haces reír,
se cubre su boca
y en ese momento puedes ver su juventud.

También es vanidosa,
con sus blusas de bolitas
y su perfume preferido.

En su jardín se la pasa
regando sus plantas,
y amanece para misa cada domingo.

Ahora, ella tiene 98 años,
y está llena de la sabiduría
de los años bien vividos.

Aunque no puede hacer
lo que hacía antes,
su amor por los suyos sigue intacto.

Superando cada generación
y sin conocer fronteras.

Generational Chains

Through the generations in our family,
        we have accumulated chains. Holding us back

from growing and thriving. These chains
        have been weighing us down for years

without anyone trying to break them apart.
        Until I came into the world. I came fighting

out of my mother's womb. Fighting
        the restraints that were placed on her.

These chains couldn't stand a chance.
        My cries were heard, my hands reached for dreams,

and my mind expanded with new ways
        to navigate the world. Once the chains broke,

no one could keep me small, with no room to grow.
        I have expanded new horizons and now can give

new visions of light for those to come.

Mi madre hizo realidad mis deseos

The other day I asked my mother,
"De niña, ¿qué querías ser de mayor?"

Ella no pudo contestar.

It made me feel sad
that she was never given the choice:
para pensar en su futuro.

Taken out of school
to do all the chores
for her brothers.

Expected to get married,
and have children
to be able to move out of her grandparents' house.

Nothing more.
Nothing less.

The thought that she could be
something más
nunca pasó por su mente.

Qué privilegio me ha dado.

To have the ability to think about mis sueños y mis deseos
before even thinking about marriage.

Qué inspiración es ella.

At times I question how I'm going to get through the days,
but she got through the days raising six girls with my father.

Hija de mi padre

Sin terminar la escuela.
Sin el apoyo de su madre y padre.

Con el estrés de tener que hacerlo
en un país con un idioma desconocido.

A woman who grew up to be
an amazing mother:

    mi hermosa madre.

El amanecer

Un regalo de Dios brillando como el sol de la mañana.
Los rayos llegan a todos los que están más allá.

Un alma del sol, que usa los rayos brillantes
para reponerse y reiniciarse.

Reiniciarse para brillar aún más,
y alumbrar a todos los que se encuentran con ella.

Como el pétalo de una flor

Soy delicada como el pétalo de una flor
que se cae mientras la lluvia la derrumba.

Quizá me caigo,
pero aún así crezco con más sabiduría.

Tomo el agua de la lluvia satisfaciendo
la sed que tenía por la vida.

Repleta para la siguiente tormenta
que viene hacia mí.

Mis raíces se fortalecen en este mundo
con la seguridad de que aún puedo seguir.

Herencias

Heredé el apellido Lara de mi padre,
>   y también la testarudez que viene de él.

Cuando mis hermanas y yo alegamos,
>   mi mamá nos recuerda: *¡Tenían que ser Lara!*

Pero eso no es lo único.

También heredé lo trabajadora, el querer ayudar a los demás
>   y lo bailadora. Y si me vez, también heredè lo físico:

las cejas más gruesas y lo peludo que era mi padre.
>   Hasta tengo el mismo pico de viuda que tenía él,

el que yo trataba de esconder desde niña.
>   Pero ahora, todo lo que heredé, lo exhibo con orgullo

porque vino de él.

Hermanas Lara

Peleamos,
y también nuestros padres pelearon.

Lo aprendimos de ellos,
pero ahora es diferente
porque peleamos la una para la otra.

Tenemos el mismo genio de mi padre
y el modo de expresar amor de mi madre.

Un poco de papá:
ningún pelo en la lengua (sin pena),
somos rápidas para expresarnos.

Cuando demostramos amor,
lo hacemos más con acciones que con palabras,
como lo hace mamá.

He notado estas cosas
desde que apá falleció,
por eso trato de decir "te quiero" con más frecuencia.

Aunque, quizás,
no lo pueden decir
todas mis hermanas.

Para mi,
es mucho más importante el amor
que el querer tener la razón.

Warrior Sister

As a first-born daughter,
she was born a warrior.

Growing up armoring herself and leaving us,
yet the tribal chains still have a hold of her.

Growing up with the same walls our ancestors built,
yet wanting to be the sister, too.

She protects us with her shield
thinking she needs to be a courageous warrior for us.

Though, all we need from her
is to be our hermana instead of our elder:

Guard down,
without holding the chains tight.

Letting go to create space
para el amor de hermandad.

Nuestra hermana amada

Ella es como la madre tierra, porque lo da todo.
        No siempre está presente, pero lo está

cuando más se le necesita. Ella va hasta el fin
        del mundo para ayudar. Y simplemente

lo hace porque ama a su familia: Papá, mamà,
        sus cinco hermanas y sus sobrinos.

La familia siempre será su prioridad.

Radio Sol

La que tocaba música
me hacía como ella quería
según mi mamá.

Pero, me acuerdo que ella y yo
éramos uña y mugre,
y no recuerdo nada malo de aquel momento.

Éramos las niñas olvidadas,
porque somos las de enmedio.

Aunque a ella no le gustó que le quité su spotlight,
ella supo que estábamos en el mismo lugar.

De mis momentos favoritos
era cuando ella ponía el radio y lo detenía en random
para que yo bailara en la canción que sonaba.

Ella también ponía su música de rock
para ver el susto que me daba
y se reía.

A ella, le gustaban los libros de Harry Potter
igual que a mí, y nos peleábamos por ellos.

Pero también me llevaba a ver películas
cada noviembre, en mi cumpleaños.

Había veces que yo no quería seguir
esforzándome en la escuela,
pero ella no me dejaba rendir.

También me recogía de la clase de baile,
aunque papá y mamá no apoyaban
que me quedara después de la escuela.

Lo hizo porque ella sabía cómo se sentía
tener que dejar ir la música.

Ella era la voz en mi radio, diciéndome:

No te rindas. Yo te apoyo aunque otros no lo entiendan.
Tú sigue.

Y todavía sigue siendo esa voz para mí.

Making Friends

Someone who feels so much
can spot someone
who is ingenuine from miles away.

It's both a blessing and a curse
because sometimes I feel so lonely.

I want to see the good in people,
but it is so hard when I pick up on the side-looks,
and the whispers coming through the wind.

I try to fit into the mold of others,
but quickly realize
I cannot play the part.

My silence may come off as rude,
but I don't want to waste my time
or play any games pretending to be someone I'm not.

I don't want to gossip
or laugh at another person's expense,

I want to build deep connections
with profound conversations.

I want to know your dreams,
your fears, your hurt, and your love.

Almas gemelas

Son únicas
a su propia manera.

Sin temor de lo que viene,
ellas pelean por lo que quieren.

Sin explicaciones, sin permiso
y sin pensar en las consecuencias.

Lo hacen con la confianza de
que la vida les dará lo que desean.

Y si es lo opuesto,
ellas saben que todo estará bien.

Juntas siempre,
sin perder sus pasos.

Ellas marchan
al ritmo de su propio tambor.

Solany Lara

Finding mi Propio Sol

I used to fear the sun's rays would burn me.

The shadows of failure and judgment overtook my light,
and everything in sight.

Until the muse within couldn't be kept in the dark.

She said,

>*¡Ya no más! It's time to find your propio, Sol.*
>*The brilliance that you are, despite the dark.*
>
>*Aunque tienes oscuridad, puedes iluminar el camino*
>*con tus fortalezas e inspirando a los demás.*
>
>*Your rays of sunshine are too bright and too warm*
>*to hide behind the shades of black.*
>
>*Enough. You've had enough of the dark.*
>*You must let yourself shine, porque tú eres Sol.*

Tierra

I sometimes feel like dirt,
and forget the honor in that.

I'm the color of Earth.

An Earth that nourishes,
but also needs nourishment.

    - A brown girl

Florecemos

Mi piel me recuerda a mis antepasados en México.
Piel de tierra y tronco de árbol que sigue dando vida.

Una cultura que se ha tratado de borrar una y otra vez,
pero aún vive más allá de la frontera.

Sigue floreciendo y plantando raíces,
sin importar el camino que tomamos.

Prosperamos donde quiera que vayamos
y sin miedo en los ojos.

Estamos recuperando nuestras voces,
esas que fueron silenciadas durante tanto tiempo.

Ya es tiempo de acabar nuestro silencio.

Written from my Soul

This pen writes my dreams,
        my failures, and my triumphs.

This pen rights my wrongs. This ink
        exposes the beauty in error.

These strokes show the effort
        and feelings that take over.

Each word picked meticulously
        to convey my story.

A story that I hope reaches you.

¿De dónde vengo?

Vengo de mis padres,
ellos que lucharon para conseguirnos
una vida mejor en Estados Unidos.

Siempre unidos
para alcanzar
el sueño Americano.

¡Sí se puede!

Más con mis padres
pude yo.

Vengo de ellos,
y sin ellos
yo no podría.

Sin sus esfuerzos,
¿qué sería
de mí?

Gracias a ellos
estoy aquí.

La Generación de Hoy

Hoy en día,
encuentras a muchos
tan involucrados sólo en ellos mismos.

Sin espacio para los demás.
se olvidan de los ancestros
y la importancia de la comunidad.

Sin darse cuenta,
que fue una comunidad
la que los creó.

Self-care no tiene que significar
olvidarte de tus raíces
y pisotear a los demás.

La vida debe ser un balance
entre honrar a tus antepasados
y a ti misma.

Y usar tus regalos,
para ayudar
a los demás.

Mis antepasados viven

I didn't get to meet todos mis abuelos.
Most did not grow viejos
to see me grow up.

Some did not get to see my padres get older.
Sickness took them too soon from us,
but they still live in me.

Abuelo Jesus lives
in the strokes of my pen on paper,
porque él también era escritor y maestro.

Abuela Agustina stares
right back at me from the mirror
with her beautiful big brown eyes and skin.

Abuelo Pancho lives
in my hard work and efforts,
as I put my heart into everything I do.

Abuela Soco aún vive,
compartiendo sus consejos, rezos y chistes
con sus nietos y bisnietos.

Aún viven mis abuelos,
en mí
y en mi modo de ser.

Growth Takes Time

You need to take your time
in order to branch out and grow.

Keep your head up.

Take those slow,
quiet steps.

Don't stumble over your roots.

Instead,
embrace them.

Let them guide you.

Spotlight

Rising to the spotlight feels like standing unclothed
        in a room full of people. You shine

like the muse that you are, yet you're more susceptible
        to criticism and judgment. You radiate love,

yet not everyone's light will be attracted to yours.
        If only they knew that you aren't in need

of their illumination. You are enough
        to set a whole room ablaze.

Not a Threat

I know exactly who I am,
but that doesn't make me
more than or less than you.

It's not my fault,
I found my light
before you.

Instead of feeling threatened
by my fire,
why don't you use it?

Ignite yourself
to shine just as bright
or brighter.

Bailadora

Sólo salí bailadora,
porque es todo lo que yo miraba mientras crecía.

Íbamos de fiesta a fiesta
cada fin de semana.

Yo me quedaba viendo a todos:
los tíos, tías, primos y primas bailando.

En pareja
o haciendo pasito tun tun.

En vez de irme a dormir en una silla como todos los niños,
yo copiaba los pasos de todos:

> mi papá y mamá bailando un poquito de todo,
> mi tío Carlos y tía Vero bailando quebradita,
> mi tío Poncho y mi tía Chagua bailando swing,
> mi tío Joel bailando sus pasos en medio del círculo,
> y mis primos y primas bailando *El Payaso de Rodeo*.

Mis primeras clases de baile
eran con toda mi familia.

Gracias a ellos saque lo bailadora,
y nunca pararé de hacerlo.

Seguiré bailando
y honrando a los que me enseñaron,
a través de mis pasos.

Yo soy Sol

My passion can feel like a burn to some
        and warmth to others.

My rays may blind you,
        but if you embrace them,

they will hug you and caress your skin.
        My light covers every surface,

leaving a mark on the world as I rise.
        Despite the clouds that surround me,

I still shine.
        Brighter than ever.

Brown Scholar

I am a Brown Scholar who often struggles
        against a system not made for me.

Whites do not want me to be educated.
        They speak against my uniqueness,

but will take from me and use it as their own.
        Sometimes, me siento que I don't belong

pero I use my voice loud and proud. Educating my own,
        so they may dismantle all stereotypes.

I don't waste my energy or time trying to convince them
        that I am worthy of their time. I am a Brown Scholar

who is worthy. For myself, mi familia
        y mi comunidad.

Light

The future is bright
if you continue to
illuminate your vision
con la luz en tu vida:

> Surrounding yourself
> with people that warm you with their luz.

> Doing the activities that ignite you
> to keep going amongst the mundane.

> Spending time outdoors to rekindle
> the inspiration in you.

> Sharing your brilliance with others,
> so they may share theirs with you, too.

Take perspective to glow like the sun.

Pregúntate,
¿qué es lo que te ilumina?

El avivamiento

Quizá me apagué por un momento
sin saber cómo seguir.

La muerte me hizo sentir
como si una parte de mí hubiera muerto con mi padre.

Pensé que mi niña interior había muerto
y que no era posible revivir y gozar mi vida.

Pero, no es cierto
porque el miedo es una mentira.

Quizás tomará tiempo
para creer que hay un arco iris al final de la lluvia,
pero estoy empezando a ver el sol.

Lo hago un poco más cada vez que creo en mí:

en mis sueños,
en mi poder,
en mi luz.

Los sueños de mi niña interior nunca murieron,
sólo olvidé que existían dentro de mí.

Es mi deber alumbrar de nuevo la llama que llevo por dentro,
para seguir creyendo que la vida todavía se puede vivir
con ojos nuevos después de la muerte.

Con tiempo y agradecimiento,
para todos aquellos que todavía están
conmigo en esta tierra.

Hija de mi padre

Y quizá, no olvidar a mi padre,
pero saber que le gustaría que tomará las riendas de mi vida,
y todo lo que me dio para seguir cumpliendo
los sueños de su pequeña Sol.

Estoy lista para abrazar a mi niña interior
y decirle:

Todo estará bien. No tengas miedo. La luz vendrá otra vez.

Acknowledgements

I want to thank mi padre, Jose Francisco Lara, who inspired me to write avidly and to find my voice again. I know you continue to make an impact in my life because I never imagined myself getting here. Somehow you have given me the strength to stand up to the fear of failure. Aquí estoy papá, logrando mis sueños para ti, para mi familia y para mí. ¡Sí se pudo! I am incredibly thankful to my family: my mother, Maria Lara, mis hermanas: Carla, Amanda, Maria del Socorro (don't kill me), Coraly and Marely. You've put up with me in so many ways as I processed dad's leave: my mood swings, my need to retreat, and my tears. You all have contributed to this by living life with me, and being there for the process. ¡Las amo un chingo!

A mi novio, Carlos Nuñez: thank you so much for your patience, your love, and for being there for me through the hardest moments I've experienced. You don't know how much you've helped me in processing grief: the space, time, and attention you give me does not go unnoticed. ¡Te amo, te amo, te amo! To my mentor and friend, Yesenia Villalobos, thank you so much for jumping into reading my poetry and writing about your own experience with parental grief. It's incredibly vulnerable, and a leap not everyone is willing to take. I'm also incredibly grateful for your friendship and love throughout the years because even though you started as my boss, I now consider you one of my closest friends. ¡Eres una chingona en todos los aspectos! To my therapist, Ashley Tierno, thank you for your listening ear and guidance to coping better with death and the aftermath. I'm so much better with your help.

To my Alegría familia, I am so thankful for your support, guidance, and love as I embarked on this journey of writing.

I especially thank Davina Ferreira, who saw the writer in me before I saw her in myself. I can't believe it, but you made me believe in myself and inspired me to keep going. Thank you to my editors: Paloma Alcantar and Camari Hawkins, who have worked tirelessly on this book. Many thanks to my illustrator, Josie Vasquez (@dichosa.art), who was the brilliant artist behind my cover and the QR code designs. She took something I had in my mind, and crafted it all just like I imagined it. To S. Salazar (@writessalazar), I'm so incredibly thankful for your guidance in all aspects: as a friend, writer, and editor. You took my work further than I imagined.

To the publications who gave me a chance prior to getting my collection out, my deepest gratitude for giving me the chance to first publish my poems with you. I'm so grateful for your faith in my work. You make me keep believing that this writer thing is possible, and to continue submitting my work. My recommendations to any writer who is seeking to publish their work to the following journals, where earlier versions of my poems first appeared:

Breadfruit Magazine: "First Generation/Primera generación," and "Mis antepasados viven"

Azahares Literary Magazine 2023: "Family Portraits"

To my readers, gracias por comprar mi libro. This is a piece of my heart. I hope it found its way to your own corazón, and I hope it inspires you to tell your own story. Es posible. Brilla como el sol que tú eres.

Hija de mi padre

Solany Lara
Writer, Poet, Educator, and Mentor

www.writtenfrommysoul.com
@writewsoul

Born and raised in Los Angeles, California, Solany Lara is a Chicana who is the product of her immigrant parents' hard work and tenacity. Working as an academic interventionist, she assists K-8 students with their literacy and math development. She loves sharing her love of reading with everyone she encounters, as she believes that reading can have a profound effect on people's lives. This has led her to pursue a Master's Degree in Library Science at San Jose State University. When she's not studying or writing, you can find her dancing, and spending time with her cat, Azul, and her big Mexican familia.